Self Esteem

A Guide to Help You Overcome Low Self Esteem and Solve Inner Conflicts to Get Your Confidence Back

Table of Contents

Introduction 1

Chapter 1...5

Low Self Esteem and Its Manifestations.................5

What is the concept of self-esteem?........................5
What are low self esteem and its manifestations? .7
Fear & Anxiety 8
Depression..9
Hypersensitivity 9
Lack of Assertiveness 10

Chapter 2..11

The Effects of having a Low Self Esteem................11

Low Self Esteem in Children 11
Low Self Esteem in Teenagers 13
Low Self Esteem in Adults 14

Chapter 3..17

Strategies for Solving Self Esteem Issues...............17

Charity Work 17
Group Therapy Sessions 18
Private Therapy Sessions 19
Animal Therapy 20
Playing With Your Child 21
Maintaining a good appearance 22
Find an engaging hobby.......................................22
Discipline Your Body 23
Learn To Say No..24
Meditation 25

Conclusion...27

Introduction

The human mind is a complex thing. Straight from birth, the human mind starts to record information. This is a continuous process. Our subconscious and unconscious minds registers every bit of information. For example, babies are aware that crying will get them attention. Similarly, a baby also learns that a mother's embrace means safety. Even when inside the mother's womb, the human mind is constantly registering data. The music that the mother listens to, the relationship between the parents, their diets and so on; all this information is stored in the baby's mind. Not only that, but it is this information that is stored in our subconscious and unconscious minds that has the biggest say in defining who we are as a person.

It should be no surprise that in developed countries, couples that are expecting make sure that the circumstances are ideal for the birth of their child. Doctors advise a mother to indulge in book reading exercises and try to solve mathematical problems. She is also advised to listen to soothing music. The father is advised to take care of the mother. The couple should refrain from fighting and keep their tones in check. All of this is important not only for the physical wellbeing of the baby but also for its metal nourishment.

The reason behind this whole routine is that the subconscious and the unconscious mind of the baby are very active during the early part of its life. And these portions of the mind determine our personalities. Psychological studies have revealed that people who struggle with low self-esteem issues usually have had bad experiences in the past. Such people have memories of traumatic experiences locked away in their unconscious mind. For example, people who were shunned by their parents/teachers during their childhood often have low self-esteem. Such people are afraid of public speaking and are very risk averse. As a result they do not developed the necessary leadership qualities and hence are overlooked for promotions/new job opportunities. So we can see the domino effect in action. Having a troubled childhood will have serious repercussions all our lives.

Thorough the course of this book, we will look at some of the major personality disorders associated with having low self-esteem. We will also take a look at the experiences and practices that lead to such behavior. Shyness, stress, fear and anxiety are all manifestations of having low self-esteem. These negative personality traits have serious repercussions on our lives. We will explore some of these underlying issues and how they can become a huge obstacle on your road to success. Towards the end, we will discuss some important techniques and mind hacks that can be used to reprogram your brain and overcome your fears. I am hopeful that you will find this book informative and it will spur you on to face your inner demons and come out victorious.

Chapter 1

Low Self Esteem and Its Manifestations

Before we can start our discussion on low self-esteem, it is important that we first grasp the concept of self-esteem. In order to understand the dynamics of human psychology, it would be beneficial for us to develop our fundamental concepts before proceeding further.

What is the concept of self-esteem?

Self-esteem is a term that describes one's perception about himself or herself. It is a measure of the personal value that and individual has and is an important personality trait. This means that this trait becomes a part of who we are as a person and determines how we will behave in a given set of circumstances.

It is not necessary that the feeling of self-worth stems just from physical beauty. It depends on the individuals themselves and how they perceive themselves. It also depends on our beliefs and values. For example, one person might have a higher sense of self-worth because of their physical appearance, whereas others might attain high self-esteem through acquisition of wealth. Similarly, some people might take confidence from their abilities, for example a gifted sportsman. It all depends on the mindset of the people and similarly there are a diverse set of circumstances that can alter feelings of self-worth.

Nathaniel Branden, a renowned Canadian-American psychologist, explained the concept of self-esteem in his book 'The Psychology of Self Esteem' (1969). The author explains the three fundamental concepts about human self-esteem. He explains that self-esteem is an important aspect of the human psyche that is essential for the growth and survival of mankind. As explained earlier, an individual's experiences in life and their social values have a lot of say about their levels of self-esteem. And in addition to that, Branden claims that a person's actions and his thoughts can also have an impact. That is why psychologists put emphasis of indulging one's mind with happy and positive thoughts. Positive thinking can bring a positive change to our lives. It can provide motivation and the will power required to excel in our practical lives.

Abraham Maslow, who is famous for his work, the Hierarchy of Needs, explains that the in order to attain real self-actualization, the human mind has two requirements. First, there should be an intrinsic sense of self-worth within a person. This is very important for personality development. And in order to strengthen this feeling of self-respect, a person needs positive reaffirmations from other human beings around them. Our level of self-esteem has a direct impact on how we behave and perform in our life. Therefore, it is imperative that we develop an understanding about its importance and learn how we can tailor it to our advantage.

What are low self esteem and its manifestations?

Now that we have developed a basic understanding about self-esteem we can take our discussion further. Self-esteem can be perceived as a continuum. It can be thought of as an independent variable on the x-axis of our graph. The dependent variable is our level of achievement. Plotting such a graph will result in a curvilinear model with the apex lying somewhere around the middle. This reveals an interesting finding. Low self-esteem as well as high self-esteem can both be disastrous. It is a general belief that excess of anything is bad. So it is as well with our issues of self-esteem. However in this book, we will focus more on the effects of low self-esteem. People with low self-esteem believe that there is something fundamentally wrong with them and that whatever they attempt to do in public would have embarrassing consequences. Thus, they have very low self-confidence and struggle to fully express themselves. Such people are often introverts and have very limited social lives.

Psychological studies have revealed that having low self-esteem can lead to the development of several negative personality traits. We will now take a brief look into some of the symptoms of low self-esteem.

Fear & Anxiety

People with low self-esteem issues often have to deal with fear and anxiety. They become overly concerned with themselves, especially when there is a need for interaction with other people. Children who suffer from low self-esteem become afraid to take part in school plays and sports. They believe that they do not have the necessary skills and confidence. Such people often have what we know as self-esteem attacks. There can be several triggers that lead to such attacks, and the affected person often becomes reclusive. The extent and duration of this state is determined by how deeply the person is affected by their fears.

Depression

Depression is another manifestation of low self-esteem. People with low self-value struggle to keep a positive frame of mind. They constantly doubt themselves and their abilities. They struggle in almost every part of their lives. For example, keeping a healthy relationship can become quite a challenge. Such people often consider themselves inferior to their partners and always suspect that they would be rejected in favor of better prospects. This state of mind leaves them dejected and hopeless. Such people are not ambitious as the fear of failure always clouds their thoughts.

Hypersensitivity

Hypersensitivity is another clear indicator of a person who is suffering from low self-esteem. Such people not only think negatively about themselves but they think that others around them feel the same way. Negative thoughts pop up in their minds. They believe that others think very little of them and see them as failures and rejects. Thus, such people are often on the lookout for indications that prove their fears. They can perceive jokes and funny comments in a very negative sense and can easily become offended by them.

Lack of Assertiveness

Having low self-esteem results in low self-confidence. Such people struggle to stand by their views and are often submissive. They might also become compulsive liars. If telling the truth would result in some kind of confrontation or unpleasant situation then these people tend to lie about their true feelings. Hence they often get stuck in abusive relationships.

These were some of the major symptoms of having a low self-esteem. Other symptoms include hypervigilance, self-sabotaging and other obsessive-compulsive disorders.

Chapter 2

The Effects of having a Low Self Esteem

Low self-esteem is an issue that can affect us at every stage of our lives. There are several examples around us where children, teenagers and adults have all struggled to cope with the repercussions of their low self-esteem. This negative personality trait should be taken seriously and efforts should be made to counteract this problem as much as possible. In order to understand the extent of the damages caused by low self-esteem, let us see how it affects our lives as children, teenagers and adults.

Low Self Esteem in Children

Having a healthy childhood both physically as well as mentally is very important. The foundation that is built in your early years should be strong and provide a solid foundation for your growth all through your life. Therefore it is important to realize the impact of low self-esteem on children.

As we discussed above, having low self-confidence breeds negative traits of anxiety, fear, self-doubt, depression and other diverse effects that can be crippling for a child's mental growth. Studies have revealed that a child with low self-confidence struggles to cope with his/her studies. They become socially reclusive and struggle to make any real friends in school. They struggle to perform tasks that require teamwork such as sports. These children rarely take part in school plays and debating competitions. The cause behind such behavior can be found hidden in the subconscious of the children. Most of the time, children with low self-esteem are often publically scolded by their parents for any mistakes that they might have made in the past. Similarly, some parents shun their children from becoming overly expressive in family gatherings. This traumatic experience is registered in the subconscious mind of the child. And thus any time they are required to address an audience, for example, their subconscious remembers that it is not supposed to open up as it is a bad thing. Hence, the child struggles to find words as they panic and are left red faced.

These children might also develop obsessive-compulsive disorders as a consequence of low self-esteem. Especially those children with a disapproving father or mother. Children who are afraid of making mistakes often resort to lying in order to avoid angering their parents. This is a very bad habit to have and it destroys the credibility of a person if he/she is caught lying.

Low Self Esteem in Teenagers

In the teenage years, it is often said that a person is ruled by his/her emotions. It can be a difficult time for some as there are a lot of physical and mental changes to cope with. Hence, a person needs to be mentally strong in order to come out of this phase unscathed. Unfortunately that is not the case for everyone.

Experts suggest that adolescent girls are more vulnerable to low self-esteem issues than boys during their teen years. However this may vary from place to place. For example, in developed countries like the United States, girls may become overly concerned with their physical appearance as they are exposed to fashion magazines that contain pictures of swimsuit models and fitness celebrities. This leads them to compare their own bodies and critique their looks. This might lead to confidence issues. Their studies can also suffer as a result. Surveys have revealed that over 70% of the girls between the ages of 15-17 in the United States avoid school activities because they feel bad about their looks. Low self-esteem is also known to be the cause of increase in teenage pregnancies.

In the developing, male dominated countries like India, adolescent boys can be affected just as much as girls of their age. In such countries the number of male students is much greater than the number of female students. Hence, teenage boys with low self-esteems develop a complex about their looks. They start to doubt themselves and envy those that have a good relationship with the opposite sex. These boys often struggle to communicate with their female classmates, often feeling flustered and annoyed with themselves. These young adults might resort to the use of steroids in order to develop their bodies and appear more appealing to the opposing gender.

These are some of the major issues that plague teenagers and immensely hamper their development.

Low Self Esteem in Adults

Just like with children and teenagers, low self-esteem has a strong impact on the adult population.

Because of their traumatic experiences, such adults have deep rooted problems that can have a dire effect on their daily lives.

Because of low self-confidence, such adults are very risk averse. They are afraid of taking bold steps and prefer to do everything by the book. They also find it difficult to communicate with others and lack decisiveness. Because of this they are not considered as suitable leaders and are often overlooked for promotions. As a result they start feeling disheartened and frustrated with themselves.

People with low self-esteem are often submissive and get stuck in abusive relationships. They are constantly ruled by the fear that if they stand up for themselves, they would have to go through a break up and then struggle to find someone new. Hence they start hiding things from their partners as well. This is the perfect recipe for disaster.

As in the case of children, adults too can develop obsessive-compulsive disorders. For example, most of us are aware of the term 'stress eating.' People with low self-esteem are often stressed out and as a result they start eating more. Obesity is one of the major problems plaguing the general population in the United States. Low self-value can also have an impact on the willpower and determination of people. Such people give up easily and find it difficult to stick to simple tasks such as exercising or dieting etc.

Chapter 3

Strategies for Solving Self Esteem Issues

Now that we have developed an understanding about some of the key issues related to low self-esteem and how it affects our lives, we can move forward and discuss some of the strategies that can be employed to counteract these issues.

Charity Work

As discussed, people with low self-esteem often have very negative thoughts about themselves. They often feel dejected and label themselves as 'good for nothing.' In order to boost their self-confidence and to address the self-hatred issues, charitable work can be quite helpful. By working with a charitable organization, orphanage, NGO or etc. an individual can actually do some good for others. This creates a sense of wellbeing and accomplishment. For example, helping raise money for the education of an orphan, helping the church or any other such activity can have a positive impact on a person's mindset. When people see the look of thankfulness and satisfaction on the faces of those they are helping, these people can't help but feel elated. Their feelings of self-hatred are somewhat subdued. Charity can go a long way into helping people with deep rooted self-confidence issues

Group Therapy Sessions

Attending therapy sessions with an expert can also be quite helpful. This allows opportunities for people to find others with a similar plight. One of the major repercussions of having low self-esteem is that people feel isolated. They believe that others around them are indifferent of their condition. Finding other people who have similar experiences can be quite relaxing. You can share your experiences and learn what strategies are being employed by others to help counter their problems. This allows the introverts to come out of their shell and express what is in their hearts.

Private Therapy Sessions

Private sessions with a therapist can also prove to be quite helpful. An experienced psychologist makes use of tried and tested exercises that are known to have an impact on the low self-esteem problem. These psychologists help people in setting up S.M.A.R.T. goals for themselves. There is a possibility that people with such issues will aspire to achieve unrealistic targets. Hence when they are unable to meet their goals, the sense of uselessness and self-doubt increases. This is something that an individual can try themselves. S.M.A.R.T. stands for:

- Specific

- Measureable

- Achievable

- Relevant

- Time Bound

This is very important because accomplishing tasks that you have set for yourself can be a real confidence booster. For example, you can convince yourself to write a book. Once you have set up your objective, try to complete it within a given timeframe. You can set the task of preparing a manuscript and then give yourself six months of time to do that. This can give you a renewed sense of purpose and you can start feeling good about yourself. Similarly, you can try and maintain a list of your strengths. Aim to add at least three strengths to your list and read that list to yourself before going to sleep. This can help condition your subconscious as the subconscious mind is most active when we are asleep.

Animal Therapy

Animal therapy has also been found to be of help to people with self-esteem issues. People who feel especially isolated and struggle to make friends can help themselves by getting a pet. Pets give unconditional love to their masters without any regard to their looks, status or any similar criteria. Experiencing such unconditional love can help people will low self-worth. They start feeling valued and find a constant companion. You can get a dog or a cat or any of the common household pets. Raising those pets and seeing their affection for you can be quite an ego boosting experience.

Playing With Your Child

As a parent, if you feel that your child is becoming a recluse and struggles to mix with other children, you can start by taking some time out of your routine to play with them. Do not worry about looking silly sitting in the sandbox or stacking blocks. Your child's mental health is more important. Also, you do not have to spend too much time with them. An hour or two each day will be more than enough to bring about a positive change in your child. Make sure to address your child with their proper name and maintain regular reaffirming touches. If your child is interested in sports, praise him/her on their effort rather than on the score. Parents can also maintain a wall of fame for their child. If for example the child is good in arts and craft, take one of their drawings and put it on their wall of fame. Similarly, if your child gets good grades in any subject, put up their report card on the wall of fame. Then whenever you have guests at your house, explain, in the presence of your child, all their accomplishments. This will help the child in developing self-confidence.

Maintaining a good appearance

Maintaining a good posture can also help you feel more confident in yourself. Practice this. Try to walk with your back straight, arms to your side and chin up. Don't walk too fast or too slow. Keep a normal pace. Similarly, practice maintaining eye contact with people when talking to them, and smile. Smiling makes you seem relaxed and approachable. People will find you friendly and confident and will treat you as such. You should also pay attention to the way you dress and how you look. Take a long look at your wardrobe. Ask your friends if you are not sure about the latest trends and then carry out a complete overhaul when required. Similarly, buy yourself a good perfume, watch or other accessories that exhibit an impressive personality. Get a decent haircut. Remember! If you dress good you look good. And when you look good you will feel good and this will result in a significant boost to your self-confidence.

Find an engaging hobby

If you have trouble talking to other people and fear making a fool of yourself during a discussion, then make sure to acquire all the knowledge that you can. Start reading books. You can pick any genre as long as you enjoy it. This will lend you some valuable perspective. Not only that, but your general knowledge will increase as a whole. Hence when you do engage in conversation with someone, you will have lots of interesting things to share with them. Your extensive knowledge on a variety of subjects (thanks to your reading habits) will surely impress your companions. They will start to value your opinions more and you will become more acceptable in the social circles. Other than that, you could perhaps start to learn some foreign language. Setting up challenging goals for yourself and then achieving those goals can prove to be quite rewarding.

Discipline Your Body

People with low self esteem are often the victims of body shaming and bullying in their childhood. If you have had similar experiences and want to do something about it then you can find solace in fitness routines. In an interview, the American sensation Ana Cheri explained to the audience how she was bullied throughout her youth and how it affected her. Then she shared with her fans how she decided to become a fitness model and how it has impacted her life. You can do something similar. Join a gym or start going for jogs in the morning. Swimming is also a very healthy activity that can have a positive influence on your body. Once you see these changes manifesting and people admiring you for them, your self-esteem issues will start to resolve. It is important to bring discipline into your life and you need to realize that if you truly want something; you have to get up and get it done.

Learn To Say No

People with self-confidence issues often lack decisiveness. They are afraid to say no to someone either from fear of hostility or from the fear of hurting someone they love. If you are plagued by a similar problem then you need to reflect on your choices. Saying yes and then cursing yourself for doing something you didn't want to will hurt both parties. You will end up doing the task assigned to you half-heartedly. This will result in a poorly executed job that might further damage your already fragile sense of self.

Hence, learn to say no. This does not mean that you have to be rude about it. Try to present your point of view with facts and logic. Make the other person realize that you won't be able to do as they ask without hurting their feelings. This is a very important skill to acquire as this will lead to developing healthier relationships. For example, you had planned a boys' night out with your friends when your girlfriend asks you to go shopping with her. You should be comfortable enough to ask your partner to postpone the shopping trip to a later date because you need some personal time. Making your partner realize the importance of personal space and giving each other some time to spend to themselves is a very healthy practice that results in long lasting relationships.

Meditation

Meditation is a powerful tool that can help relax your mind and body. It allows you to achieve a state of tranquility and gives you the chance to reflect on your life. Stuck in the cares of this world, we often forget to appreciate the little things in our life. These things might seem little to us and we often take them for granted, but they do in fact have a huge impact on your life. You can either indulge in meditation alone or join a yoga group, for example. The most important thing is to feel comfortable in order to really benefit from this activity.

Conclusion

The importance of having a positive sense of self cannot be underestimated. Our mental health is just as important as our physical health. In every stage of our life, it is important that we maintain a high self-esteem. It fuels our desires and our ambitions and gives us the confidence to go out and get things done.

Low self-esteem is an issue that should not be taken lightly. The foundations are laid down since childhood. Thus, it is extremely important that parents pay close attention to the mental wellbeing of their children. They should always be available to provide emotional comfort and reaffirmations to their children. Similarly, we should also pay special attention to teenagers. Student counselors, parents and teachers need to work together in order to win the trust of their children. Teenagers are prone to unexpected reactions because they go through a lot during puberty and often have conflicted opinions about things.

Using some of the strategies we have discussed above, you can exercise some control over your self-esteem issues. Just remember that where there is a will there is a way. You just need to wake up every day with a goal to become better than what you were yesterday.

Printed in Great Britain
by Amazon